Young Minds, Big Startups

A Beginner's Guide to Entrepreneurship

Vandana Verma

DIAMOND BOOKS

www.diamondbooks.in

Publisher : **Diamond Pocket Books (P) Ltd.**
X-30, Okhla Industrial Area, Phase-II
New Delhi-110020
Phone : 011-40712200
E-mail : wecare@diamondbooks.in
Website : www.diamondbooks.in
Edition : 2025
Printed By : Repro (India)

Preface

Welcome to Young Minds, Big Startups – A Beginner's Guide to Entrepreneurship. This book is crafted especially for high school students who are curious about the world of startups, innovation, and building something meaningful from scratch.

In today's fast-changing world, young people are not just job seekers — they are becoming job creators. This book introduces you to the exciting journey of startups: how they are born, how they grow, and how they change the world. It aligns with the National Education Policy (NEP) 2020, NCF 2023, and CBSE Skill Modules, offering not just knowledge, but hands-on thinking, real-life stories, and tools to help you explore your ideas.

Whether you dream of launching your own app, starting a food delivery business in your town, or creating eco-friendly products — this book is your launchpad.

Let this be the beginning of your entrepreneurial journey. Read it. Reflect on it. Use it to spark your ideas and fuel your future.

-Vandana Verma

Foreword

India has become a land of ideas, innovation, and ambition. With over 1.57 lakh startups and 100+ unicorns, our country is now a global leader in entrepreneurship. This incredible growth is not just driven by experienced professionals — it's being powered by students, young innovators, and teenagers just like you.

This book is a celebration of that energy. It is your guide to understanding what startups are, how they grow, and why they matter to your future and India's future. It simplifies the complex world of funding, government schemes, digital innovation, and startup stories — making it approachable for every high school student.

May this book inspire you to be curious, courageous, and creative. The world needs your ideas.

Let's build the future — one startup at a time.

Contents

Chapter 1

What is a Startup?

Have you ever thought of a smart solution to a daily problem—like an app that reminds you to drink water or a service that helps school kids recycle notebooks? What if you could turn that idea into something real, something that people use every day? That's exactly how many startups are born.

A startup is more than just a business. It's an idea in action. It's a bold attempt to change the way something works—faster, better, or smarter.

In this chapter, we will explore what startups really are, how they're different from regular businesses, why they matter to India, and how you, as a student, are already a part of this exciting world just by being curious and creative.

What is a Startup?

A startup is a newly created business that is built to solve a problem in an innovative way. It often begins with a small team of people who believe in an idea and are willing to take risks to make it work.

Startups usually:
• Use technology to deliver their product or service
• Grow rapidly by reaching more users quickly
• Aim to disrupt traditional ways of doing things
Unlike a regular shop or company that aims for stable profits over the long term, startups are designed for speed, scale, and change.

Difference Between Startups and Traditional Businesses

Aspect	Startup	Traditional Business
Focus	Innovation & solving a unique problem	Profit-making with tested business models
Speed of Growth	Rapid and scalable	Gradual and steady
Use of Technology	High	Low to moderate
Risk Level	High	Medium to low
Funding Sources	Investors, venture capital, crowdfunding	Loans, personal savings
Example	Ola, BYJU'S, Meesho	Kirana stores, clothing boutiques

Why Do Startups Exist?

Startups usually emerge when someone asks:
"Why hasn't anyone solved this yet?"

They are designed to:
• Challenge the old ways of doing things (e.g., Ola vs. taxi stand)
• Create solutions to problems (e.g., Practo for online doctor appointments)
• Bring convenience and new experiences (e.g., Zomato food delivery)

Startup = Innovation + Risk + Speed

To build a startup, one needs:
- **Innovation:** A fresh idea, product, or approach
- **Risk-taking:** The courage to fail and try again
- **Speed:** The ability to move fast, learn, and grow

The early stages of a startup are full of uncertainties. But that's also what makes them exciting!

The Indian Startup Journey: A Quick Look

India's startup scene really took off after 2014. Several key moments sparked the boom:
- Launch of the Startup India Initiative in 2016
- Explosive growth in internet and smartphone use
- Rise in venture capital and angel investors
- Government's push for Digital India

Now, India is the third-largest startup ecosystem in the world—behind only the US and China. That's a big deal!

Key Milestones in India's Startup Journey

- **2008–2010:** Flipkart begins, opening doors to e-commerce
- **2014–2016:** Ola, Zomato, BYJU'S grow rapidly
- **2016:** Launch of Startup India
- **2021:** India crosses 50 unicorns
- **2023–2024:** Over 1.57 lakh startups recognized by DPIIT

Startups are Changing India

Startups are doing more than just business. They are solving problems like:
- Access to education (BYJU'S, Vedantu)

- Urban transport (Rapido, Bounce)
- Financial services (PhonePe, Cred)
- Healthcare access (1mg, PharmEasy)
- Farming challenges (DeHaat, AgroStar)

And they're doing all this while creating millions of jobs, inspiring youth, and helping India go digital.

Startups and the NEP 2020

The National Education Policy (NEP) 2020 focuses on making students:

- Think critically
- Solve real-world problems
- Build creative solutions
- Learn by doing, not just reading

It encourages the entrepreneurial mindset—the same spirit that drives a startup founder.

Initiatives like:

- Atal Tinkering Labs
- Innovation Hubs in Schools
- Coding from Grade 6 onwards
- Entrepreneurship in curriculum

...are helping young minds like you start thinking like founders!

Case Example: A Student Startup Idea

Imagine Riya, a 15-year-old who sees how difficult it is for her classmates to recycle notebooks. She comes up with an app that lets schools collect used notebooks, recycle them, and redistribute to NGOs. She shares the idea with her science teacher, builds a team, joins a school hackathon, and soon gets selected for a city-level incubator.

That's a startup journey starting in school!

Common Traits of Startup Founders

Startups are built by people who:

- See problems as opportunities
- Don't wait—they act
- Embrace failure as a part of learning
- Build teams and networks
- Are always curious and creative

You don't need to be a tech genius to start a startup. You need a problem-solving mindset and the drive to build something better.

Fun Fact: Who Can Start a Startup?

Anyone!

- A school student
- A college dropout
- A working mom
- A retired army officer
- A group of best friends

All you need is an idea + action = impact!

Summary – Let's Wrap It Up

- A startup is a new, fast-growing business solving a real-world problem with innovation.
- Startups differ from traditional businesses in their focus on speed, scale, technology, and risk.
- India has seen a startup boom since 2014 and is now the third-largest startup hub globally.
- NEP 2020 encourages entrepreneurial thinking from school level

through coding, innovation labs, and creativity.
• Anyone with an idea and courage can become a young founder.

Activity: Think Like a Founder

Your Task:
1. What is one problem in your school, neighborhood, or city that you wish someone would solve?
2. Write down an idea you have to fix it.
3. What would you name your startup?
4. What would your first step be in turning it into reality?

Pro Tip: Share your idea with a friend or teacher. They might want to be your co-founder!

Chapter 2

The Indian Startup Ecosystem

An Overview

Imagine hundreds of students like you across India turning their ideas into apps, services, or solutions that solve real problems—from clean water in villages to AI tutors for schoolchildren. That's the energy of India's startup ecosystem.

India isn't just growing startups; it's growing an entire support system that helps young minds become entrepreneurs. This support system is called a startup ecosystem.

What is a Startup Ecosystem?

A startup ecosystem is like a team sport—it takes more than just a founder to build a successful startup.

It includes a network of:

- Entrepreneurs with ideas
- Investors who provide funding
- Incubators & accelerators that guide and mentor

• Colleges, schools, and innovation labs
• Government schemes and policy support
• Media, role models, events, and platforms

These players work together to help startups grow from an idea into a business, just like a seed needs water, sunlight, and soil to grow into a tree.

How Big is India's Startup Ecosystem?

India's startup landscape has seen explosive growth in the last decade.

Some mind-blowing numbers:
• Over 1.57 lakh startups recognized by DPIIT (as of Dec 2024)
• India ranks 3rd globally after the US and China
• Around 111 unicorns (startups worth over $1 billion)
• More than 17.28 lakh jobs created
• Startups present in 650+ districts
• Growth rate of 12–15% year-on-year

It's not just about numbers—it's about the impact these startups are making in education, health, finance, agriculture, and more.

What Makes India a Hotspot for Startups?

India has several strengths that fuel this growth:

Factor	Impact
Young population	Median age is 28 – millions of energetic, creative minds
Digital access	900M+ internet users; cheap data costs
Government support	Startup India, Digital India, NEP 2020, etc.
Funding	Global & Indian venture capital flowing in

Innovation infrastructure	Incubators, Atal Tinkering Labs, hackathons
Tier-II and Tier-III city participation	More inclusive, grassroots innovation

These factors make India not just a land of consumers but a land of creators.

India's Major Startup Hubs

While startups are spreading to every corner, some cities have emerged as powerful hubs:

City	**Nickname**	**Key Sectors**
Bengaluru	Startup Capital of India	SaaS, AI, EdTech, DeepTech
Delhi-NCR	Policy & Consumer Hub	FinTech, HealthTech, AgriTech
Mumbai	Financial Capital	MediaTech, FinTech, D2C brands
Hyderabad	Innovation Hotspot	Biotech, EV, Analytics
Pune, Chennai, Kochi	Emerging Players	Robotics, AgriTech, Cleantech

Smaller towns like Jaipur, Indore, Surat, and Bhubaneswar are also witnessing a startup surge, proving that innovation is no longer limited to metros.

Sectors Driving India's Startup Growth

Startups are active in every sector. Here are some leading ones:

1. **EdTech**
   - **Solves:** Quality education access, exam prep, skill learning
   - **Examples:** BYJU'S, Unacademy, Vedantu

2. **FinTech**
   - **Solves:** Payments, loans, credit access, insurance
   - **Examples:** PhonePe, Razorpay, Cred

3. **HealthTech**
   - **Solves:** Telemedicine, e-pharmacies, diagnostics
   - **Examples:** Practo, 1mg, PharmEasy

4. **AgriTech**
   - **Solves:** Market access, irrigation, crop advisory
   - **Examples:** DeHaat, Kheyti, AgroStar

5. **Cleantech & EVs**
   - **Solves:** Clean energy, transport, climate tech
   - **Examples:** Ather Energy, BluSmart, ReNew Power

6. **DeepTech & AI**
   - **Solves:** Core R&D, automation, data science
   - **Examples:** Niramai (AI for cancer), GreyOrange (robotics)

Startup India & DPIIT

In 2016, the Indian government launched Startup India, a flagship initiative to:

- Simplify business registration
- Offer tax benefits and funding
- Promote innovation through incubators and mentors

Startups registered under the Department for Promotion of Industry and Internal Trade (DPIIT) enjoy:

- Easy patent filing

• Access to government tenders
• Tax exemptions
• Faster regulatory approvals

This has led to a startup boom like never before!

The Rise of Unicorns and Soonicorns
• A unicorn is a startup valued at $1 billion or more.
• A soonicorn is a startup on its way to becoming a unicorn.
• A zebra is a startup that grows sustainably and values both profit and purpose.

India has:
• 111 unicorns as of 2024
• Over 355 soonicorns in the pipeline

Examples of Indian unicorns: Zomato, Paytm, OYO, Swiggy, Razorpay, Lenskart, Zepto

Technology: The Backbone of the Ecosystem

Technology is making it easier than ever to:
• Launch ideas with low cost (via cloud, no-code tools)
• Reach users digitally
• Collect feedback instantly
• Scale fast using data & AI

Thanks to Jio, India Stack, Aadhaar, and UPI, even a street vendor in a village can accept digital payments and register a business.

Youth Are Leading the Way
• India has the world's largest youth population.
• Many successful founders are in their teens and early 20s.
• College campuses are full of hackathons, innovation labs, pitch fests.

• Students are learning coding, design thinking, problem-solving from early grades.

This young energy makes India's startup ecosystem vibrant and future-ready.

Role of Schools and NEP 2020

The National Education Policy 2020 promotes:
• Critical thinking and entrepreneurship
• Vocational learning and skill-building
• Coding and AI learning from Grade 6
• Setting up Atal Tinkering Labs in schools

Students today are not just job seekers—they're job creators. Schools are becoming startup nurseries.

Rural Startups and Tier-II Success Stories

Startups are no longer a metro-only story.
• Over 51% of startups now come from smaller cities.
• Sectors like agriculture, handlooms, and rural e-commerce are seeing innovation.
• Digital access is turning local problems into global opportunities.

Example: An app in a Tier-II town connects artisans with global buyers.

Challenges to Overcome

Despite the growth, some challenges remain:
• Funding access for early-stage ideas
• Infrastructure in smaller towns
• Lack of mentorship in rural areas
• Complex regulations in some sectors

However, the government and private sector are working to fix these through:

- Grant schemes
- Incubator networks
- Online mentorship platforms
- Startup-friendly policies

Snapshot: India's Startup Ecosystem at a Glance

Metric	Figure (2024)
Total startups	1.57 lakh+
Unicorns	111
Recognized districts	650+
Jobs created	17.28 lakh+
Annual growth	12–15%
Female-led startups	20 unicorns

Summary – Key Takeaways

- A startup ecosystem includes founders, investors, mentors, incubators, and government programs.
- India is the third-largest startup ecosystem globally, with over 1.57 lakh recognized startups.
- Major hubs include Bengaluru, Delhi-NCR, Mumbai, but Tier-II cities are rising.
- **Top sectors:** EdTech, FinTech, AgriTech, HealthTech, Cleantech.
- Youth and technology are key forces behind the boom.
- India's policy environment and infrastructure are evolving to support more innovation.

Activity: Explore Your Startup City

Instructions:

1. Choose any Indian city (metro or small town).

2. Research:

- o At least 2 startups from that city
- o What sector they belong to
- o What problem they solve

3. Reflect:

- o What makes this city a good place for startups?
- o Could your idea work there too?

Present your findings in a 1-page mini-report or slide.

Chapter 3

Types of Startups in India

Close your eyes and think of the word startup. What comes to mind? Maybe an app like Swiggy or an edtech platform like BYJU'S? But did you know that startups are not all tech companies?

Some grow organic vegetables, while others build electric scooters. Some are trying to improve the lives of farmers, while others create fashion for the future.

That's the beauty of the startup world—it's diverse, dynamic, and driven by ideas.

In this chapter, we will explore the different types of startups based on what they sell, how they operate, what drives them, and the impact they want to make. You'll also meet real examples from India's growing startup universe.

Why Understanding Startup Types Matters

Knowing the type of startup you want to build or work for helps in:

- Identifying your strengths (tech vs. creative vs. social change)
- Finding the right co-founders or investors

• Understanding business models and funding options
• Making better career and entrepreneurship choices

1. Based on Product vs. Service

Type	What It Offers	Example
Product-based	Sells physical or digital products	boAt (earphones), Ola Electric (EVs), Zepto (quick delivery)
Service-based	Offers solutions, consulting, platforms	Urban Company (home services), Practo (health consults)

Product-based startups involve creating a tangible item—something people can use, wear, drive, or download. This may require more upfront investment in design and manufacturing.
Service-based startups, on the other hand, solve problems through experiences. Think of booking a cab, scheduling a tutor, or fixing a leaky tap.
Many successful startups use a mix—for example, BYJU'S sells both content (a product) and tutoring sessions (a service).

2. Based on Tech vs. Non-Tech
Not all startups need to write code or build apps.

Let's break them down:
A. Tech-based Startups
• Use digital tools, apps, websites, or AI/ML to solve problems
• Scalable with less physical infrastructure
• **Example sectors:** FinTech, EdTech, SaaS, HealthTech

Examples:
• Zerodha (online trading platform)
• Niramai (AI for breast cancer detection)

• Dunzo (hyperlocal delivery app)

B. Non-Tech Startups
• Focus on physical goods, services, or offline experiences
• Rely more on logistics, branding, or manual operations

Examples:
• Bira91 (craft beer brand)
• WOW! Momo (QSR food chain)
• Nua (women's hygiene products)

Many non-tech startups still use technology for operations, marketing, or logistics. The lines are blurring!

3. Based on Profit Orientation

Type	Goal	Examples
For-Profit	Generate revenue and grow market share	Flipkart, Nykaa, Lenskart
Non-Profit / Social Impact	Focus on solving social issues, not profits	Goonj (rural clothing), Kheyti (climate-smart farming)
Hybrid	Combine revenue with impact	SELCO (solar for rural India), Agastya Foundation (STEM education in rural areas)

Social impact startups may not make big profits, but their success is measured in lives changed or communities empowered.

Today's students are increasingly interested in purpose-driven entrepreneurship—making a difference while also being sustainable.

4. Based on Business Model

Startups can also be categorized by how they make money or operate:

A. B2C – Business to Consumer

• Sells directly to customers
• Focuses on user experience, branding, fast growth
• **Example:** Swiggy, Meesho, Boat

B. B2B – Business to Business

• Sells to other businesses
• Requires strong networking, fewer clients but bigger deals
• **Example:** Zoho, Freshworks, RazorpayX

C. D2C – Direct to Consumer

• Avoids middlemen like shops or distributors
• Mostly e-commerce or social media-led
• **Example:** Mamaearth, Wakefit, Noise

D. Marketplace Models

• Connects buyers and sellers, charges commission or listing fee
• **Example:** Ola, Flipkart, UrbanClap

5. Based on Scale and Stage

Type	Meaning	Examples
Bootstrap	Self-funded by founders	Zerodha
Seed-stage	Initial funding stage	College ideas, competitions
Growth-stage	Rapid user/customer growth	CRED, ShareChat
Unicorn	Valued at $1 billion+	Swiggy, BYJU'S, OYO

Soonicorn	Close to becoming a unicorn	Apna, Dunzo, Teachmint
Zebra	Grows steadily, sustainable, and ethical	Kheyti, Agastya Foundation

Not all startups aim to be unicorns. Zebras are rising as examples of sustainable, ethical businesses.

6. Based on Industry Sector

India has startup activity in 50+ sectors!

Here are some key categories:

Sector	What It Solves	Example Startups
EdTech	Learning access & quality	BYJU'S, PhysicsWallah
FinTech	Payments, loans, credit	PhonePe, Razorpay
HealthTech	Remote care, diagnostics	Practo, 1mg
AgriTech	Farming solutions	DeHaat, AgroStar
DeepTech	Core science & R&D	Niramai, GreyOrange
CleanTech	Solar, EVs, climate tech	Ather Energy, ReNew Power
SpaceTech	Private satellites, launch tech	Skyroot, Agnikul
D2C Brands	Lifestyle, beauty, wearables	Mamaearth, Lenskart

Each of these has its own growth curve, investors, and government schemes.

7. Based on Founder Demographics

Startups are now being categorized based on who is founding them:

A. Women-led Startups

- 20 of India's 111 unicorns are women-led
- Women now lead startups in fashion, health, tech, and social impact

Examples:

- Nykaa – Falguni Nayar
- Sheroes – Sairee Chahal
- YourStory – Shradha Sharma

B. Student/Teen-led Startups

- Students are launching real businesses before graduation!

Examples:

- Tilak Mehta (Papers N Parcels, age 13)
- Shravan & Sanjay Kumaran (GoDimensions, age 10 & 12)

Real-Life Indian Examples by Category

Startup	Category	Highlight
Zomato	B2C, Tech-based, Unicorn	Food delivery, IPO in 2021
boAt	Product-based, D2C	Top-selling earwear brand
BYJU'S	EdTech, Unicorn	World's most valuable edtech
Kheyti	Social Impact, AgriTech	Greenhouse-in-a-box for farmers
Mamaearth	D2C, Sustainability	Natural beauty products
Apna	Soonicorn, Employment	Jobs for blue-collar workers

Skyroot Aerospace	SpaceTech	India's private satellite launcher

Summary – Key Takeaways

• Startups can be product-based or service-based, tech or non-tech, and for-profit or impact-focused.
• Business models include B2B, B2C, D2C, and marketplace.
• Founders today include students, women, and rural innovators.
• India has a wide range of sectors—from EdTech to SpaceTech—each offering cpportunities.
• Unicorns, Soonicorns, and Zebras show different paths to startup success.

Activity: Classify Your Dream Startup

Task:
• Think of a startup idea (real or imaginary).

• **Classify it under the following:**
1. Product or service?
2. Tech or non-tech?
3. For-profit or impact-driven?
4. Sector it belongs to
5. Would it be B2B, B2C, or D2C?

Example:
• **Startup Name:** BookLoop
• **Product or Service:** Service
• **Tech or Non-Tech:** Tech-based (app)
• **Profit Model:** For-profit, student discounts
• **Sector:** EdTech
• **Model:** B2C
Share your idea with your class or innovation club and get feedback!

Chapter 4

Meet the Young Founders

What were you doing at age 13? Maybe juggling school and hobbies? Now imagine starting a company that delivers packages across a city. That's what Tilak Mehta did. All over India, teenagers and college students are proving that age is just a number when it comes to launching a startup.

In this chapter, we'll meet some inspiring young founders—students and teens—who saw a problem and built real-world solutions. Their journeys show that passion, curiosity, and courage can lead to amazing results, even before turning 18.

Why Focus on Young Entrepreneurs?

India has the largest population of youth in the world, and they are:

- Tech-savvy
- Problem solvers
- Social media natives
- Driven to create impact

With support from parents, schools, and mentors, many of them are building startups while still in school or college. Their ideas range from apps to agriculture, from logistics to education.

Common Traits of Young Founders

1. They solve personal problems.
Most startup ideas come from challenges they face at school, home, or in their communities.

2. They use technology creatively.
Even without coding expertise, they use available tools to build something new.

3. They learn by doing.
Young founders are not afraid to fail. They launch fast, learn fast, and grow fast.

4. They build teams early.
Friends become co-founders. Teachers become mentors. Networks matter.

Real-Life Stories of Young Indian Founders

1. Tilak Mehta – *Founder of Papers N Parcels (Age: 13)*

Problem Solved: Tilak forgot his books at a relative's house and couldn't find a quick courier solution.

Solution: He launched Papers N Parcels, a startup that delivers documents and small parcels within Mumbai in a few hours using Mumbai's dabbawala network.

Achievements:
• Built a team of 200+

• Uses tech + traditional delivery
• Became a TEDx speaker

2. Shravan and Sanjay Kumaran – *Founders of GoDimensions (Ages: 10 & 12)*

City: Chennai

Startup: Mobile app development company focused on education and games.

Achievements:
• Created over 11 apps
• Invited to present at Apple Inc.
• One of India's youngest CEO and CTO pairs

3. Harshwardhansinh Zala – *Founder of Aerobotics7 (Age: 14)*

City: Gujarat

Startup Focus: Building drones that detect and defuse landmines.

Impact: Worked with the Indian Army to explore real-world defense applications.

Recognition: Signed a ₹5 crore MoU with Gujarat government in 2017.

4. Sreelakshmi Suresh – *India's Youngest Web Designer (Age: 8)*

City: Kozhikode, Kerala

Startup: Created websites for schools and businesses under eDesign.

Specialty: She made her first website at age 6 and launched a company at 11.

Awards: National Child Award for Exceptional Achievement

5. Ajay Bansal – *Founder of Smart Stick for the Blind (College Student)*

City: Haryana

Invention: A walking stick that uses sensors to help visually impaired people avoid obstacles.

Support: Received funds and incubation support under Atal Innovation Mission.

Impact: Helps make mobility easier for visually impaired users.

6. Ananya Jain – *Founder of FullCircle (Age: 20)*

City: Delhi

Startup Focus: Biotech startup that recycles human hair into useful products like fertilizers and eco-friendly plastic.

Recognitions:
- TEDx speaker
- Represented India at global forums
- Inspired by sustainability goals

7. Trisha Prabhu – *Founder of ReThink (Teen Founder, NRI from India)*

Focus: Anti-cyberbullying software

Impact: Warns users before they post hurtful comments online

Recognition: Global Innovation Awards, praised by Google & UN

8. Ritesh Agarwal – *Founder of OYO Rooms (Started at Age 19)*

Though not a teen, Ritesh is India's most famous young entrepreneur.

Idea: Affordable, standardized hotels for budget travelers

Support: Won the Thiel Fellowship and dropped out of college

Today: OYO is one of India's biggest unicorns

Patterns Across These Stories

- Started with a simple idea
- Built a team or asked for help
- Used school projects or competitions as launchpads
- Faced challenges like funding, balancing studies, or being taken seriously
- Found mentors and believed in themselves

How Did They Get Noticed?

1. School or college innovation competitions
2. Youth entrepreneurship platforms
3. Startup India events
4. Social media + news coverage
5. Support from family, teachers, and incubators

Challenges Faced by Young Founders

Challenge	**How They Overcame It**
Age bias	Built strong pitches, showed proof of concept
Lack of money	Entered contests, used crowdfunding

Time pressure	Managed studies and startup as a team
Technical limitations	Learned online, partnered with coders
Fear of failure	Treated failure as learning

Support Systems That Helped

• **Atal Innovation Mission (AIM):** Offers labs, mentors, and grants to student innovators
• **Startup India:** Provides access to incubators and recognition
• **School innovation clubs:** Allow idea testing in safe spaces
• **Parents and teachers:** Encouragement plays a major role
• **Youth platforms:** Youth Ideathon, Young Entrepreneurs Academy, etc.

Key Learning from Their Journeys

1. Start small, think big – Even a school project can become a million-dollar startup.
2. Age doesn't limit impact – Some of the most original ideas come from young minds.
3. Solve for your world – The best ideas come from things you care about.
4. Build confidence, not just code – Communication, leadership, and empathy matter.

Spotlight: Girl Power in Startups

Girls across India are launching impactful businesses:
• **Aarushi Bansal (Age 15):** Started a menstrual hygiene awareness app
• **Riya Jain (Age 16):** Launched an eco-friendly jewellery brand
• **Shrishti Bakshi:** Walked 3800 km across India to promote digital literacy for women

More support from schools, families, and mentors is encouraging girls to take the leap into entrepreneurship.

Summary – Key Takeaways

• Young founders in India are launching powerful startups in tech, health, environment, and education.
• Age is not a barrier—some kids start at age 10 or younger.
• Their success comes from observing everyday problems, being curious, and building a team.
• Support from schools, parents, and platforms like AIM and Startup India helps them grow.
• Their journeys inspire other students to explore entrepreneurship early.

Activity: Your Founder Story

Imagine this:
You are 15 years old and have just launched your own startup!

Answer the following:
• What problem are you solving?
• What's your startup called?
• Who is your co-founder?
• How will your product/service help others?
• What challenges do you expect?

Share your story with your classmates. Vote for the most creative, practical, and impactful idea!

Chapter 5

How Startups Get Funded

The Money Game

You've got a startup idea. You've created a prototype, maybe even gained your first few users. Now comes the big question: How do you get money to grow it?

Welcome to the world of startup funding—a vital part of every entrepreneur's journey. Whether it's borrowing from family, convincing investors on Shark Tank, or launching an IPO on the stock exchange, startup funding follows certain stages and strategies. In this chapter, we break down the funding process in simple terms, from bootstrapping to billion-dollar valuations.

Why Do Startups Need Funding?

Startups need capital for many reasons:

- To build a product or service
- To hire a team
- To market their idea

• To scale up and reach more users
• To buy equipment, software, or inventory

Without funding, even great ideas may never reach their full potential.

Stages of Startup Funding

Startups usually grow through different funding stages, based on their development.

1. Bootstrapping – Funding it Yourself
• The founder uses personal savings or borrows from family and friends.
• **Pros:** Full control over your business
• **Cons:** Limited growth; personal financial risk

2. Seed Funding
• First external investment to validate the idea and build a prototype.
• **Sources:** Angel investors, seed funds, or startup competitions
• **Amount:** ₹5 lakh to ₹1 crore

3. Series A Funding
• The startup has users, data, and wants to expand.
• Investors look for a strong team and scalable product.
• **Amount:** ₹5 crore to ₹20 crore+

4. Series B, C, D...
• Funding continues in rounds as the startup grows.
• Used for national expansion, hiring leadership, international launches, or R&D.

5. IPO (Initial Public Offering)
• The company is listed on the stock market.
• Anyone can buy shares.

• **Example:** Zomato and Nykaa launched IPOs in India in 2021.

Infographic Idea: Funding Journey of a Startup

Stage → Funding Source → Objective
• Bootstrapping → Personal → Build MVP
• Seed Round → Angel Investors → Test the market
• Series A → Venture Capital → Scale product
• Series B+ → Institutional Investors → Expansion
• IPO → Public → Raise large capital, exit for early investors

Who Provides the Money?

1. Angel Investors
• Wealthy individuals who invest in early-stage startups.
• Offer mentorship and networking in addition to money.
• **Examples:** Kunal Bahl (Snapdeal), Rajan Anandan (Peak XV)

2. Venture Capitalists (VCs)
• Firms that invest large sums into startups with high growth potential.
• Take equity (ownership percentage) in exchange for funding.
• **Examples:** Sequoia Capital, Accel, Tiger Global

3. Incubators & Accelerators
• Help startups grow through mentoring, training, and small funds.
• Incubator = early idea stage
• Accelerator = scaling up fast
• **Examples:** Y Combinator, T-Hub (Telangana), NSRCEL (IIM-Bangalore)

4. Government Grants and Schemes
• Support from Startup India, Atal Innovation Mission, etc.
• No equity needed; often targeted at student and social impact startups.

5. Crowdfunding

- Public contributes small amounts online to support a startup.
- **Popular platforms:** Kickstarter, Ketto, Milaap
- Ideal for social ventures or creative projects

6. Bank Loans and NBFCs

- Loans for businesses that meet eligibility criteria.
- Involve interest payments and credit checks.
- Options include MUDRA loans for micro-startups

Equity vs. Loan – What's the Difference?

Feature	Equity Funding	Loan Funding
Money From	Investors (VCs, Angels)	Banks or NBFCs
Repayment	No repayment, give equity	Monthly EMIs
Ownership Change	Yes – you give shares	No change in ownership
Risk	Shared with investor	Entire risk on you
Example	Shark Tank investment	MUDRA loan

Pitching Your Startup

To raise funds, startups must pitch their idea. A pitch is a short,

powerful presentation that tells potential investors:

- What your startup does
- What problem it solves
- Who your customers are
- Why your idea is different or better
- How you'll use their money

Most pitches also include:

- Revenue model
- Market opportunity
- Team details
- Funding requirement and equity offered

The Perfect Pitch Deck – 10 Slides

1. Problem
2. Solution
3. Market size
4. Product demo
5. Business model
6. Competitors
7. Go-to-market strategy
8. Team
9. Financial projections
10. Ask (how much money, for what purpose)

Famous Indian Startups & Their Funding

Startup	First Funding Stage	Notable Investors	Total Raised
BYJU'S	Seed (2011)	Sequoia, Tencent	$5.7 Billion
Zomato	Series A (2013)	Info Edge, Ant Group	$2.1 Billion
Ola	Seed (2011)	SoftBank, Matrix	$3.8 Billion
Zerodha	Bootstrapped	None (Self-funded)	$0 (profit)
Ketto	Crowdfunding	Public via donations	₹110+ crore raised

Student Startups and Funding

Did you know many student startups get funds even before graduating?

Platforms that help include:
- IIT, IIM Incubators
- Youth Ideathon (CBSE)
- Atal Incubation Centres
- Startup India's Seed Fund Scheme
- Campus Angel Networks

Startups like Notebook (e-learning), Clairco (air quality tech), and Agrowave (agri supply chains) began in college and received early grants or angel funding.

Success Tip: Use Competitions & Grants First

Before jumping into VC pitches:
- Win school/college innovation contests
- Apply for government schemes
- Join startup bootcamps
- Build a Minimum Viable Product (MVP)

These steps give you credibility, early feedback, and confidence.

Mistakes First-Time Founders Make

- Asking for too much money too soon
- Giving away too much equity
- Not having a business model
- Not knowing the numbers (cost, revenue, profit)
- Not having a clear "problem-solution" fit

What If I Don't Want Investors?

Not all startups need outside money. Some founders prefer to bootstrap:
- Keep ownership
- Grow slowly but steadily
- Stay debt-free

Zerodha, Zoho, and Wingify are profitable bootstrapped startups in India.

Reflection Exercise: Funding Pathway

Choose a startup idea (real or imaginary), then answer:

- Will you start with bootstrapping, crowdfunding, or a grant?
- What would you name your startup?
- What is your funding goal?
- Would you offer equity or prefer a loan?
- Who would you pitch to first?

Summary

- Startups go through multiple funding stages: bootstrapping, seed, series A/B/C, and IPO.
- Investors include angel investors, VCs, banks, and even the public (crowdfunding).
- Equity involves giving up a portion of ownership; loans require repayment.
- A pitch is how you convince others to invest in your vision.
- Many student startups today are gaining funds through competitions and government support.

Chapter 6

Startup India & Government Support

What happens when a country decides to support its young entrepreneurs not just with words, but with action, funding, policies, and training? It creates a movement—one that transforms the economy and empowers a generation. That's exactly what Startup India, a flagship initiative of the Government of India, aims to do. Launched in 2016, Startup India has played a key role in making India one of the top three startup ecosystems in the world. In this chapter, we'll explore how the government supports startups, which schemes students and young founders can access, and why public support matters for entrepreneurial success.

What is the Startup India Initiative?

Startup India is a government program launched on January 16, 2016 by Prime Minister Narendra Modi.

It aims to:

- Build a strong startup culture across India
- Simplify processes and reduce regulations

• Provide financial and infrastructural support
• Inspire youth to create jobs, not just seek them

This initiative works under the Department for Promotion of Industry and Internal Trade (DPIIT), which also officially recognizes startups under certain eligibility criteria.

As of December 2024, India has over 1.57 lakh DPIIT-recognized startups across 650+ districts, creating more than 17.28 lakh jobs.

Key Components of Startup India

Startup India is not just a slogan—it is a structured framework. It offers:

1. Startup India Hub
A one-stop platform for startup guidance, **connecting:**
• Entrepreneurs
• Incubators
• Accelerators
• Mentors
• Government departments

You can explore this hub at www.startupindia.gov.in

2. Self-Certification Compliance
Startups can self-certify under 6 labor laws and 3 environmental laws. This means less paperwork and fewer inspections during the early years—saving both time and money.

3. Startup India Portal & Mobile App
This digital platform helps startups:
• Apply for DPIIT recognition
• Access funding and learning modules
• Participate in startup events, hackathons, and challenges

Startup Funding Schemes by the Government

The government supports startups with financial assistance through dedicated schemes.
Here are some important ones:

1. Startup India Seed Fund Scheme (SISFS)
- **Launched:** 2021
- **Purpose:** To provide financial assistance for proof-of-concept, prototype development, product trials, market entry, and commercialization.
- **Fund:** ₹945 crores allocated
- **Who can apply:** DPIIT-recognized startups via incubators

2. Fund of Funds for Startups (FFS)
- **Managed by:** SIDBI (Small Industries Development Bank of India)
- **Purpose:** Provides funding to SEBI-registered Venture Capital funds, which then invest in startups.
- **Total allocation:** ₹10,000 crores
- **Startups funded so far:** Over 900

3. MUDRA Loan Scheme
- **Launched by:** Ministry of Finance
- **Purpose:** Offers micro-financing to small businesses and entrepreneurs
- **Loan Types:** Shishu (up to ₹50,000), Kishor (₹50,000–₹5 lakh), Tarun (₹5–10 lakh)
- **Beneficiaries:** 69% of recipients are women entrepreneurs

4. Stand-Up India Scheme
- **Launched:** 2016
- **Target Group:** SC/ST and Women entrepreneurs
- **Loan:** ₹10 lakh to ₹1 crore
- **Goal:** To promote inclusive entrepreneurship at the grassroots

5. ASPIRE Scheme

• **Full Form:** A Scheme for Promotion of Innovation, Rural Industries and Entrepreneurship

• **Focus:** Promoting startups in agro-based industries and rural areas through incubation centres

6. TIDE 2.0 (Technology Incubation and Development of Entrepreneurs)

• **Launched by:** Ministry of Electronics and IT

• **Purpose:** Supports startups working in tech-driven areas like IoT, AI, blockchain, and robotics

• **Includes:** Grants, mentorship, lab support, and prototyping aid

Atal Innovation Mission (AIM)

One of the most powerful government-led programs to inspire innovation is the Atal Innovation Mission.

Subcomponents:

1. Atal Tinkering Labs (ATLs):

- o Set up in schools to encourage innovation and critical thinking
- o Students get access to 3D printers, robotics kits, electronics, and problem-solving challenges

2. Atal Incubation Centres (AICs):

- o Set up in universities to nurture early-stage startups
- o Offers mentorship, co-working space, and seed funding

3. Atal Community Innovation Centres (ACICs):

- o Focused on rural and underserved regions
- o Helps local innovators scale their ideas into businesses

State-Level Support: Local Startup Missions

Beyond the central government, many states have launched their own startup programs:

State	Program	Key Features
Kerala	Kerala Startup Mission (KSUM)	Incubators, youth challenges, seed fund
Telangana	T-Hub	India's largest innovation campus
Gujarat	iCreate	International partnerships, investor summits
Karnataka	Elevate 100	Grants for top 100 startups annually
Tamil Nadu	Startup TN	Focus on Tier-II and rural startups
Odisha	Startup Odisha	Startup Yatra, seed funding, innovation zones

These state-level initiatives are crucial in decentralizing the startup movement beyond metros and reaching smaller towns and villages.

Intellectual Property Support for Startups

Ideas and innovations need protection. That's where Intellectual Property Rights (IPR) come in.
The government offers:

1. SIPP Scheme (Startup Intellectual Property Protection)
- 80% rebate on patent filing
- 50% rebate on trademark filing
- Access to expert facilitators

2. Support for International Patent Protection in Electronics &

IT (SIP-EIT)

- Reimbursement of international patent filing costs
- Focused on tech startups

These programs encourage startups to protect their innovations and compete globally.

Table: Key Government Schemes for Startups

Scheme Name	Focus Area	Benefit
SISFS	Seed stage startups	₹20 lakh for prototype, ₹50 lakh for marketing
MUDRA	Micro/small businesses	Loans up to ₹10 lakh
FFS	VC Fund support	Indirect funding via VC funds
Stand-Up India	Women & SC/ST entrepreneurs	₹10 lakh – ₹1 crore loan
ASPIRE	Rural/agro startups	Incubation, skill training
TIDE 2.0	Tech startups	Grants + incubation
SIPP	IP protection	Patent/trademark cost rebates
Atal Innovation Mission	Innovation at all levels	ATL, AIC, ACIC

Government & School-level Initiatives

The National Education Policy (NEP) 2020 has emphasized entrepreneurial learning from early grades.

Programs like:

- Innovation & Entrepreneurship Clubs in schools

• Business Plan competitions at the district and national levels
• Exposure visits to startup hubs (like T-Hub or IIT incubators)
• Teacher training on startup mentorship

...are now part of regular curriculum or co-curricular activities.

Success Stories Backed by Startup India

Some startups that benefited from government schemes include:

• Ather Energy (EV) – TIDE 2.0 + FFS
• Niramai (HealthTech) – SISFS
• Agnikul Cosmos (SpaceTech) – Startup India recognition + IP support
• Coconut Homes (AgriTech, Kerala) – KSUM grant
• FIA Tech (FinTech) – MUDRA and SIDBI support

These stories prove that even the biggest ideas often begin with small but well-supported steps.

Summary

• Startup India is a powerful government initiative launched in 2016 to nurture entrepreneurship in India.
• The program offers funding, mentorship, compliance relief, and training to startups at all stages.
• Students and young innovators can access school-based labs, seed grants, and competitions.
• Central and state governments provide many schemes including SISFS, MUDRA, ASPIRE, and Atal Innovation Mission.
• Intellectual property support and startup hubs across India are accelerating startup growth.

Reflection Activity: Your Startup, Your Support

Task: Pick a startup idea that you have or admire. Then:

1. Identify one central government scheme and one state-level initiative that could help it grow.
2. Write 3 reasons why government support is important for new businesses.

“What if your idea could create jobs, help people, and change the world—wouldn’t you want all the help you can get?”

Chapter 7

Digital India and the Startup Boom

Imagine a world where you can pay your school fees, order lunch, attend a live class, and consult a doctor—without stepping out of your home. In India, this is not just a possibility but a daily reality. Thanks to Digital India, a nationwide movement to transform the country into a digitally empowered society, startups have found the perfect launchpad to grow fast and reach millions.

In this chapter, we'll explore how Digital India, powered by tools like UPI, Aadhaar, India Stack, and the internet revolution, has become the backbone of India's startup boom.

What is Digital India?

Digital India is a flagship initiative launched by the Government of India in 2015. Its goal is to ensure that every citizen can access digital services, information, and resources through affordable internet and digital infrastructure.

The three main vision areas of Digital India are:
1. Digital infrastructure as a core utility to every citizen
2. Governance and services on demand
3. Digital empowerment of citizens

For startups, this means better access to:
• Online platforms
• Cloud-based services
• Digital payments
• e-Governance tools
• Transparent and paperless systems

How Digital India Supports Startups

Digital India has created a strong foundation for startups to launch, operate, and scale rapidly. Here's how:

1. Aadhaar – A Unique Digital Identity
• Every Indian citizen now has a 12-digit biometric identity.
• Startups use Aadhaar for eKYC (Know Your Customer), helping verify identities in seconds.
• This makes it easier to onboard users, customers, and even employees.
Example: Fintech startups like Paytm and PhonePe use Aadhaar to verify users quickly and securely.

2. UPI – Unified Payments Interface
• Launched in 2016, UPI allows instant money transfers using mobile phones.
• UPI has transformed India into a cashless economy, supporting both small vendors and large companies.
• In 2024 alone, UPI recorded over 11 billion transactions per month.
Example: A tea seller in a village now accepts digital payments via UPI. This opens up a whole new customer base for rural entrepreneurs.

3. India Stack – A World-Leading Digital Infrastructure
India Stack is a set of APIs and digital layers that allow governments, businesses, startups, and developers to use India's digital identity and transaction systems.

It has four main components:
• Presenceless Layer: Aadhaar for identity
• Paperless Layer: DigiLocker, eSign for digital documents
• Cashless Layer: UPI, BHIM for digital payments
• Consent Layer: Account Aggregator framework for secure data sharing

Why It Matters: India Stack has made India the first country to build public digital infrastructure that startups can use at almost no cost.

4. ONDC – Open Network for Digital Commerce
• ONDC is a government-backed initiative to democratize e-commerce.
• It allows small businesses to list their products on an open network without depending on Amazon or Flipkart.

Example: Startups in Tier-II and Tier-III cities now have a national reach without spending big on marketing.

5. TIDE 2.0 and MeitY Support
• The Ministry of Electronics and IT (MeitY) supports Technology Incubation and Development of Entrepreneurs (TIDE).
• It funds early-stage startups, especially those working in AI, blockchain, and IoT.

Impact: Startups working on digital innovations can receive mentorship, funding, and infrastructure support from over 50+ TIDE centres across India.

The Internet Revolution: Jio, Smartphones & Data Boom

In 2016, the launch of Reliance Jio changed India forever. Here's how:

- Cheapest internet rates in the world
- High-speed 4G networks across rural and urban areas
- Over 900 million internet users in India by 2024

This affordable access has fueled:

- Digital learning platforms like BYJU'S, Unacademy
- HealthTech startups offering telemedicine
- AgriTech solutions using mobile apps for farming advice
- Job platforms for blue-collar workers

Case Study: How UPI Fueled Startup Growth

Let's take the example of Cred, a startup that rewards users for paying credit card bills on time:

- It uses UPI for bill payments and user engagement.
- Gained millions of users due to fast, secure digital transactions.
- Became a unicorn in just three years.

Other UPI-powered startups:

- **Razorpay:** Helps small businesses accept digital payments.
- **PhonePe:** Offers mobile recharges, insurance, and gold investment.

Without UPI and India Stack, these startups would have spent years and millions building their own payment infrastructure.

Inclusion of Tier-II and Tier-III Startups

Digital India has helped startups emerge in smaller towns like:

- Jaipur (FinTech, EdTech)
- Kochi (Cleantech, Marine Tech)
- Nagpur (AgriTech)

• Indore (D2C brands)

These cities now have:
• Internet access
• Incubation hubs
• Local investor interest
• Government-supported startup missions
Fact: Over 51% of India's startups today come from non-metro

Digital Learning and Innovation

NEP 2020 emphasizes Digital Literacy and Entrepreneurial Thinking in schools:
• Atal Tinkering Labs in 10,000+ schools
• Coding, AI, and Robotics curriculum from Grade 6 onwards
• Virtual internships and digital career platforms

This means students can:
• Start learning business skills early
• Access mentors online
• Join startup competitions and pitch events digitally

Data Snapshot: India's Digital Impact

Metric	Value (2024)
UPI transactions/month	11+ billion
Internet users	954 million
Tier-II/III startup share	51%
Government Digital Initiatives	50+ schemes
Aadhaar coverage	99%+ of adult population

The Mindset Shift

Thanks to shows like Shark Tank India, entrepreneurship is now dinner-table talk.

Even students in schools are learning:
• How to pitch
• How to build MVPs (Minimum Viable Products)
• How to create digital content for their business ideas

With tools like Canva, ChatGPT, YouTube, and Zoom, even a solo student entrepreneur can build a mini company from a smartphone.

Global Recognition

India's Digital Public Infrastructure is now a model for the world. Countries in Africa, Southeast Asia, and Latin America are exploring similar models.

Quote by the World Bank (2023):
"India Stack has revolutionized digital access for the poor and set a global benchmark in digital public goods."

Summary

• Digital India has created the foundation for startups through internet access, digital payments, Aadhaar, and India Stack.
• UPI, ONDC, and Aadhaar have made transactions fast, easy, and secure.
• Affordable smartphones and Jio's data revolution expanded startup reach to smaller towns.
• Government programs like TIDE 2.0 and MeitY support tech innovation.
• NEP 2020 and Atal Labs are preparing students for digital entrepreneurship.

• India’s digital model is now inspiring the world.

Activity: Build a Digital Startup Plan

Imagine you are launching a new digital service for your school or town.

Answer the following:

• What is the service or app about?
• How will you use UPI, Aadhaar, or ONDC?
• What will your app/website look like?
• What problem are you solving?

Sketch out your idea, and pitch it to your class or family!

Chapter 8

The Entrepreneurial Mindset

Do You Have It?

Imagine being the captain of your own ship—setting your course, steering through storms, and discovering new lands. That's what being an entrepreneur feels like.

But before you launch your startup or build your big idea, there's something even more important to develop—your mindset.

Entrepreneurship is not just about having a great idea. It's about the way you think, learn, and act. In this chapter, we'll explore the mindset that powers successful founders, why failure isn't the end, and how you can start training your brain to think like a true innovator.

What is an Entrepreneurial Mindset?

An entrepreneurial mindset is a way of thinking that helps you identify opportunities, take risks, solve problems creatively, and learn from your experiences—especially the failures.

Think of it like a toolkit in your brain that includes:
• Curiosity – Always asking "Why?" and "What if?"
• Resilience – Bouncing back from failures and setbacks
• Initiative – Taking action without waiting for someone else to tell you what to do
• Empathy – Understanding what people need and how to help them
• Adaptability – Changing your plan when things don't work out
• Creativity – Thinking outside the box
• Leadership – Inspiring and working with others

Why Mindset Matters More Than Ideas

A good idea is just the starting point. Many successful entrepreneurs had average ideas but **a strong mindset that helped them:**
• Improve the idea
• Build a team
• Convince others to join
• Keep going when things got tough

That's why mindset > idea.
You might have heard of famous founders like Steve Jobs (Apple), Elon Musk (Tesla/SpaceX), or Kiran Mazumdar-Shaw (Biocon). What made them stand out wasn't just what they built—it was how they thought, persisted, and adapted.

Growth Mindset vs Fixed Mindset

Psychologist Carol Dweck talks about two types of mindsets:

Growth Mindset	Fixed Mindset
"I can learn anything with effort"	"I'm either good at it or not"
"Mistakes help me grow"	"If I fail, I'm not good enough"
"I'll try new strategies"	"This is too hard"

“Feedback helps me improve”	“I hate being corrected”

Entrepreneurs always operate with a growth mindset. They see failure not as defeat but as data—something that helps them improve their next step.

Learning from Failure

Failure is not the opposite of success—it’s a part of it.

Here’s how successful founders handle failure:

• Tilak Mehta (Papers N Parcels) had delivery challenges when he started. He didn’t quit—he refined his system.

• Elon Musk had rockets explode. He kept building.

• BYJU’S started as offline classes. When that model failed to scale, it pivoted online.

Ask any entrepreneur, and they’ll tell you their biggest lessons came from things not going according to plan.

Pro tip: Keep a “Failure Journal” where you write down what went wrong and what you learned from it.

Skills That Shape the Entrepreneurial Mindset

You don’t need to be born an entrepreneur—you can train your brain for it. **Let’s explore key skills:**

1. Design Thinking

A problem-solving approach used by innovators like Apple and Google.

Steps include:

1. Empathize – Understand the user’s problem
2. Define – Narrow down the challenge

3. Ideate – Brainstorm multiple solutions
4. Prototype – Create a small version of your idea
5. Test – Try it out and learn from feedback

Design thinking encourages experimentation and keeps the user at the center.

2. Storytelling
Can you explain your idea in 60 seconds? Can you inspire someone to join your mission?

Storytelling is powerful. Every pitch, investor presentation, or team meeting uses this skill. Practice explaining your ideas clearly, using real-life examples and emotions.

3. Teamwork
No startup is built alone. Entrepreneurs need to:
• Listen actively
• Share responsibilities
• Respect differences
• Resolve conflicts

Great founders make everyone feel like a co-founder.

4. Basic Tech Skills
You don't need to be a coder—but understanding basic digital tools, spreadsheets, websites, and automation gives you a huge advantage. Even better if you're curious about AI, data, or app-building!

How Schools Can Nurture This Mindset

Thanks to NEP 2020, schools are starting to create a culture of creativity and innovation:
• Atal Tinkering Labs (ATL) offer robotics kits, sensors, and DIY tools

• Startup Clubs host idea challenges and mentor talks
• Entrepreneurship Subjects are part of CBSE skill education
• Youth Ideathons invite students to submit business ideas and win seed funding

If your school doesn't have these yet—be the first to propose them!

Famous Quotes That Reflect the Entrepreneurial Mindset

• "I have not failed. I've just found 10,000 ways that won't work." – Thomas Edison
• "You miss 100% of the shots you don't take." – Wayne Gretzky
• "The biggest risk is not taking any risk." – Mark Zuckerberg
• "Be the change you want to see in the world." – Mahatma Gandhi

These quotes are more than words—they're mental fuel for entrepreneurs.

Reflection Activity: My Founder Journal

Take a moment to reflect and write in your personal Founder Journal:

1. What's one problem in your life you wish had a better solution?
→ **Example:** "Too many students are confused about career options."

2. What's a simple idea you could test to solve it?
→ **Example:** "A quiz app that suggests careers based on hobbies and skills."

3. What scares you the most about starting something new?
→ **Example:** "What if people laugh at my idea?"

4. What's one small action you can take today?
→ **Example:** "Talk to 3 friends and ask what career advice they wish they had."

The key is to start—no matter how small.

Summary

• An entrepreneurial mindset is about how you think, not just what you do.
• Key traits include curiosity, resilience, empathy, creativity, and leadership.
• A growth mindset helps you learn from failure and keep improving.
• Skills like design thinking, storytelling, and teamwork make a big difference.
• Schools, policies, and communities can nurture entrepreneurship from a young age.
• You can begin shaping your mindset today by reflecting, exploring, and taking action.

Chapter 9

Building Your First Startup

Student Edition

So far, you've learned what startups are, how they grow, where they get support, and the mindset of successful founders. Now it's time for you to start thinking like one. This chapter is your startup starter kit—a student-friendly guide to building your own venture from scratch.

No matter your age, location, or experience, every big idea starts small. Let's break it down into simple, doable steps so you can start your journey as a young entrepreneur!

Step 1: Find a Problem Worth Solving

Every great startup begins with a problem. That's the core of entrepreneurship—solving something real.

Ask yourself:

- What do you and your friends complain about often?
- Is there a gap in your school or city services?

• Can you improve something you use daily—like study apps, public transport, or mess food?

Tip: A good problem is something specific, relatable, and frequent.

Example:

Problem: Students forget homework deadlines.
Startup Idea: A fun, gamified app that reminds students and awards points for completing work early.

Step 2: Brainstorm a Startup Idea

Now, think of solutions. Your idea doesn't need to be complicated—it just needs to be clear and useful.

Ask:
• What's the simplest way to solve this problem?
• Will this help more people than just me?
• Can it be built with low cost or free tools?

Tip: Think "MVP" – Minimum Viable Product. Start small, test fast.

Example:
Idea: An Instagram page to promote local handmade crafts from your neighborhood.
Later, it could become a full e-commerce store!

Step 3: Choose a Co-founder or Team (Optional)

Startups are hard to build alone. You might want a co-founder—someone who shares your passion and complements your skills.

Think about:
• Who is good at coding, writing, or design?

- Who brings energy and ideas?
- Who is trustworthy and consistent?

Tip: Many successful startup duos are built on friendships and shared goals!

Step 4: Name Your Startup

Time to get creative! A good name is:
- Short and easy to remember
- Related to your idea
- Available as a domain (optional)

Try tools like:
- NameMesh
- Shopify Name Generator
- Domainr

Activity: Write 5 possible names and ask friends which one they remember best.

Step 5: Make a Simple Business Plan

Don't worry—you don't need a 50-page document. Start with a Startup Idea Canvas that **answers these:**

Question	Your Answer
What problem are you solving?	
Who is your target audience?	
What is your product/ service?	
How will you reach your users?	

What makes you unique?	
How will you make money (if any)?	

Tip: Your business plan should evolve as you learn. It's okay to change.

Step 6: Build Your Prototype

Now it's time to build something real—a basic version of your idea.

For a tech idea, this could be:
• A simple website using tools like Wix, WordPress, or Google Sites
• A working app prototype using MIT App Inventor or Thunkable

For a product:
• Create samples using home materials or 3D printing
• Take photos and explain its use

For a service:
• Run a small pilot with 3–5 users and collect feedback

Reminder: Start simple. The goal is to test and learn, not be perfect.

Step 7: Pitch Your Startup

Your idea matters—but how you present it matters more. That's where a good pitch comes in.

The Elevator Pitch Formula:
"My startup [Startup Name] helps [target users] solve [problem] by providing [solution]. It is unique because [what makes it stand out]."

Example:
"My startup ExamEase helps students manage exam stress by

offering AI-powered revision tools. Unlike other apps, we customize each plan based on learning habits."

Step 8: Get Feedback and Improve

Ask teachers, parents, friends, or mentors to:
• Try your prototype
• Tell you what works and what doesn't
• Suggest improvements

Tip: Treat feedback as a gift. Even criticism helps you grow. Use what you learn to make version 2.0 better!

Step 9: Share Your Work

Don't keep your idea a secret. Show it off!

Where to share:
• Instagram reels or YouTube videos
• Local school exhibitions or science fairs
• Startup pitch contests for students
• Online platforms like Github, Behance, or your own blog

You might even catch the attention of a local investor or startup mentor!

Step 10: Celebrate and Keep Learning

Whether your idea becomes a real business or not, what you've done is amazing.
You've:
• Identified a real-world problem
• Built a solution
• Created a plan
• Taken the first steps

This is what entrepreneurs do. The more you try, the better you'll get.

Worksheet: Startup Idea Canvas

Copy this template and fill it out with your own idea:

Section	Your Answer
Startup Name	
What problem are you solving?	
Who are your target users?	
What is your solution?	
How are you different from others?	
How will you test your idea?	
What tools will you need?	
Who is on your team (if any)?	
How will you share or launch it?	

Bonus: Add a simple logo and tagline!

Pitch Practice: The 60-Second Pitch

Time yourself and answer these questions aloud:

- What's your startup about?
- Why did you start it?
- How does it work?
- Who is it for?
- What's next for your idea?

Practicing this builds confidence—and prepares you for real opportunities like contests or Shark Tank-style events.

Summary

• You can start a startup even as a student—begin with a problem worth solving.

• Use tools like Startup Idea Canvas and Elevator Pitch to structure your idea.

• Build simple prototypes using free tools and test with users.

• Feedback is your friend—improve, pitch, and keep evolving.

Reflection Activity: Your Founder Journal

Start your own "Founder Journal" and write down:

1. One problem in your daily life
2. A possible solution you could offer
3. Sketch or describe your product/service
4. A catchy name and pitch
5. What support you would need to launch

Who knows? This could be the first page of your startup story.

Chapter 10

The Road Ahead

Careers & Resources in Startups

You've learned what startups are, how they grow, who funds them, and even how students can launch their own ventures.
But what if you don't want to start your own company—yet still want to be a part of the exciting startup world?

Good news: startups need talented, curious, and driven people to help them grow. Whether you're interested in design, coding, marketing, data analysis, or even storytelling, there's a place for you in this fast-growing ecosystem.
This chapter will help you explore the career opportunities, skill paths, and resources that can connect you to the startup world.

Why Work in a Startup?

Working in a startup is different from working in a traditional company.
Here's why:

Startup Jobs	Traditional Jobs
Fast-paced and dynamic	Structured and process-driven
Flexible roles (you do many things)	Defined roles (you do one main thing)
Steep learning curve	Slow and steady learning
Direct access to founders	Multiple management levels
Impact from Day 1	Results take time to show

Startups are a great place for students and freshers because they offer real responsibility and hands-on experience from the beginning.

Exciting Careers in Startups

Here are some of the most in-demand roles in the startup world today. These are not just tech jobs—**they span across many interest areas:**

1. Product Manager (PM)

• Think of this person as the captain of the ship.

• They decide what features to build, when to launch, and how to improve the product.

• **Skills Needed:** Problem-solving, user research, communication, basic tech knowledge.

2. UI/UX Designer

• Designs how an app or website looks and feels.

• Works to make apps easy and fun to use.

• **Skills Needed:** Creativity, design tools like Figma/Adobe XD, user testing.

3. Software Developer / Engineer

• Builds the actual product – apps, platforms, and features.

• Backend and frontend roles available.

• **Skills Needed:** Coding (Java, Python, JavaScript), debugging, logic.

4. Marketing & Growth Hacker

• Helps the startup grow its user base using creative online methods.
• Social media, content marketing, and influencer partnerships are key tools.
• **Skills Needed:** Communication, creativity, analytics, digital tools.

5. Data Analyst

• Interprets numbers to help startups make better decisions.
• Tracks user behavior, sales, and performance.
• **Skills Needed:** Excel, SQL, Python, data visualization (e.g., Tableau).

6. Customer Success / Support Executive

• Keeps customers happy and loyal.
• Solves issues and explains the product features.
• **Skills Needed:** Empathy, problem-solving, communication.

7. Content Creator / Storyteller

• Writes blogs, records videos, manages social media.
• Tells the startup's story to the world.
• **Skills Needed:** Writing, video editing, creativity, audience understanding.

8. Finance & Operations Associate

• Manages budgets, resources, payments, and backend operations.
• Keeps the engine running smoothly.
• **Skills Needed:** Math, Excel, understanding of finance or logistics.

Skills That Will Help You Shine

No matter what job you pick in a startup, some universal skills can **help you stand out:**

• Communication – to explain ideas clearly.
• Teamwork – startups need everyone working together.
• Critical Thinking – for solving unique challenges.

• Curiosity – to keep learning and improving.
• Ownership – to take charge and act like a mini-CEO.

Bonus Tip:
Startups love people who are proactive. Don't wait to be told what to do—suggest ideas, test them, and learn from feedback!

Pathways to Enter the Startup World

1. Internships in Startups
Start with a summer internship in a local or online startup. **Many platforms post these:**
• Internshala
• AngelList Talent
• LinkedIn Jobs
• T-Hub Intern Portal (Telangana)
• Startup India Intern Portal
These opportunities help you understand how startups work and build your resume.

2. Startup Events & Hackathons

Participate in:
• Startup pitch fests
• Hackathons
• Youth entrepreneurship summits
• Student innovation challenges
These events are great places to showcase your ideas, meet founders, and even get job or internship offers.

3. School & College Clubs

Many schools and colleges now have:
• Innovation clubs
• Entrepreneurship cells (E-cells)

• Atal Tinkering Labs
• Startup incubation centres
Be an active part of these! They often provide mentorship, networking, and even seed funding.

4. Create Your Own Project

Want to stand out? Start a mini project:
• Launch a newsletter
• Build a mobile app
• Run a small social media brand
• Sell something online

Even if it's small, it shows initiative, leadership, and entrepreneurial spirit—something every startup loves.

Helpful Resources for Teen Entrepreneurs

Books
• Zero to One by Peter Thiel
• The Lean Startup by Eric Ries
• Start With Why by Simon Sinek
• How I Braved Anu Aunty and Co-Founded a Million Dollar Company by Varun Agarwal
• Rework by Jason Fried & David Heinemeier Hansson

YouTube Channels
• Backstage with Millionaires (Indian startups)
• Whiteboard Friday (marketing tips)
• Startup Stories India
• Y Combinator (Startup advice)

Websites & Tools
• startupindia.gov.in
• nasscom.in

- YourStory.com
- Canva (for design)
- Notion (for planning)
- Figma (for UI design)

Career Alignment Exercise

Step 1: Pick 3 startup careers you're curious about.

Step 2: Match them with your hobbies/skills:
- Love writing? → Content creator
- Good with logic? → Developer or analyst
- Enjoy planning events? → Operations or product management

Step 3: Explore how to learn more:
- Find a mentor
- Take a short online course (e.g., Coursera, Udemy)
- Ask your teacher or school counselor for opportunities

Summary

- Startups offer exciting career opportunities across fields like tech, marketing, design, and operations.
- You don't need to be a founder to thrive in the startup ecosystem.
- Internships, events, clubs, and personal projects are great ways to get started.
- Focus on developing 21st-century skills like problem-solving, communication, and creativity.
- Explore resources like books, websites, and YouTube channels to keep learning.

Final Reflection

"In the startup world, age doesn't matter—your ideas and actions do."

What kind of startup would you love to work for? Write down:

• The type of product or service it offers
• The role you'd want to play
• What problem it helps solve

This is your roadmap to joining the world of startups—not just as a founder, but as a future builder!

Bonus Chapter

Top 5 Books, YouTube Channels & Websites for Teen Entrepreneurs

So, you've learned what startups are, explored real success stories, understood funding, and even started shaping your own startup idea. But how do you keep learning and growing as a young entrepreneur? Don't worry—we've got your back!
This bonus chapter gives you a goldmine of resources that will inspire, educate, and guide you in your startup journey. Whether you love reading, watching videos, or browsing websites, there's something here for every kind of learner.

Top 5 Books Every Teen Entrepreneur Must Read

These books are simple, fun, and packed with wisdom from startup founders, innovators, and thinkers:

1. "Start It Up: The Complete Teen Business Guide" by Kenrya Rankin
• Why it's awesome: This is a practical guide written specifically for teenagers. It explains how to choose a business idea, create a plan, and launch your product or service.
• What you'll learn: Business planning, budgeting, branding, and marketing.
• **Perfect for:** Middle and high school students starting their first business.

2. "The Lean Startup" by Eric Ries
• Why it's awesome: It teaches how to start small, test ideas quickly, and grow efficiently using real data.
• What you'll learn: MVP (Minimum Viable Product), iteration, and scaling.

• **Perfect for:** Teens interested in tech, apps, and product-based startups.

3. "Kid Start-Up" by Mark Cuban, Shaan Patel & Ian McCue
• Why it's awesome: Co-authored by Shark Tank investor Mark Cuban, this book motivates kids and teens to turn their ideas into income.
• What you'll learn: Real-life success stories, business basics, and confidence building.

• **Perfect for:** Young dreamers who want real, relatable advice.

4. "Be a Young Entrepreneur" by Adam Sutherland
• Why it's awesome: It's colorful, visual, and designed for younger readers, with quick facts and step-by-step advice.
• What you'll learn: Brainstorming ideas, money management, and branding.

• **Perfect for:** Visual learners and early high school students.

5. "How I Built This" by Guy Raz (Teen Edition)
• Why it's awesome: Based on the popular podcast, this book shares inspiring journeys of founders who built big brands.
• What you'll learn: Real struggles, creative thinking, and resilience.

• **Perfect for:** Teenagers looking for inspiration and role models.

Top 5 YouTube Channels for Young Entrepreneurs

Sometimes, it's easier (and more fun!) to learn by watching. These YouTube channels are perfect for visual learners:

1. Young Entrepreneurs Forum
• Why follow: Offers simple and motivational business ideas with how-to guides.

• What to watch: "Top 10 Business Ideas for Students" and "How to Start with Zero Investment."

2. Shark Tank India – Official Channel
• Why follow: Real entrepreneurs pitching their businesses to investors. Great for understanding what makes a business idea work.
• What to watch: Pitches by college students and feedback from sharks.

3. Nas Daily
• Why follow: Short, global stories about innovation, people, and change-makers.
• What to watch: Stories about unique startups and creative solutions.

4. TED-Ed / TEDx Talks for Youth
• Why follow: Engaging videos on creativity, innovation, and leadership.
• What to watch: "Why You Will Fail to Have a Great Career" by Larry Smith and "The Power of a Young Entrepreneur."

5. Startup Stories – Inspiring Journeys
• Why follow: Biographies and case studies of global founders like Elon Musk, Steve Jobs, and Indian entrepreneurs.
• What to watch: "The Story of Paytm," "The Story of BYJU'S," and "How Zomato Started."

Top 5 Websites and Platforms to Explore

These websites offer tools, mentorship, learning courses, and startup competitions you can actually be part of:

1. Startup India (www.startupindia.gov.in)
• Why visit: It's the official portal by the Government of India for startup support.
• What to do: Register a startup, join events, apply for funding

schemes like SISFS, and learn through their "Learning & Development" modules.

2. Atal Innovation Mission (aim.gov.in)

• Why visit: Supports school-level innovation through Atal Tinkering Labs (ATLs).

• What to do: Join or start a tinkering lab in your school, participate in student innovation competitions.

3. T-Hub (www.t-hub.co)

• Why visit: India's largest incubator supporting student-led startups.

• What to do: Attend webinars, join mentorship programs, and see success stories.

4. NASSCOM 10,000 Startups (10000startups.com)

• Why visit: Helps tech startups connect with investors, mentors, and customers.

• What to do: Access free resources, startup accelerators, and startup bootcamps.

5. Youth Ideathon (youthideathon.in)

• Why visit: India's largest K–12 student innovation challenge.

• What to do: Pitch your startup idea, get mentoring, and win prizes. Many students go on to launch real businesses!

Bonus Tools for Student Founders

• Canva (www.canva.com) – Make pitch decks, logos, posters, and social media posts.

• Google Workspace – Use Google Docs, Sheets, Slides for business planning and collaboration.

• Trello / Notion – Organize tasks and projects for your team.

• LinkedIn – Build your professional profile and follow startup founders and communities.

Final Reflection: Your Entrepreneurial Toolkit

You now have a solid starter pack to continue your journey as a young entrepreneur. Whether you enjoy reading books, watching real founder journeys, or participating in startup events—use these resources to build your skills and confidence.

Quick Challenge:

- Choose 1 book, 1 video, and 1 website from the list above.
- Write down 3 things you learned from each.
- Think about how you'll apply those insights to your own idea.

Wrap-Up: You're Just Getting Started!

Remember, the world of startups is not just for adults—it's for YOU. Your ideas matter. Your passion matters. Your journey starts now, and every book you read, every pitch you watch, every idea you write down brings you one step closer.

As we say in startup lingo: "Execute, iterate, and grow!"

Glossary

Key Terms from This Chapter

Term	Meaning
Startup	A newly formed company aiming to solve a problem with an innovative solution.
MVP (Minimum Viable Product)	The simplest version of a product that can be released to test an idea.
Pitch	A short presentation where a founder explains their business idea to investors or judges.
Incubator	A program that supports early-stage startups with resources and mentoring.
Accelerator	A time-bound program that helps startups grow quickly with mentoring and funding.
Unicorn	A privately-held startup valued at over $1 billion.
Angel Investor	A person who provides money and guidance to early-stage startups.
Entrepreneurship	The act of starting and running your own business.
Innovation	Using creativity to solve problems in new and better ways.
Digital Public Infrastructure (DPI)	Technology systems like Aadhaar, UPI, and India Stack that enable digital services.